2/02

OTHER PEOPLE'S TROUBLES

PHOENIX POETS

A SERIES EDITED BY ALAN SHAPIRO

JASON SOMMER

other,
people's
troubles

THE UNIVERSITY OF CHICAGO PRESS *Chicago & London*

Jason Sommer teaches creative writing and literature at Fontbonne College in St. Louis, Missouri. He is the author of a book of poems titled *Lifting the Stone* (1991).

The University of Chicago Press, Chicago 60637
The University of Chicago Press, Ltd., London
© 1997 by The University of Chicago
All rights reserved. Published 1997
Printed in the United States of America

06 05 04 03 02 01 00 99 98 97   1 2 3 4 5

ISBN 0–226–76815–5 (cloth)
      0–226–76816–3 (paper)

Library of Congress Cataloging-in-Publication Data

Sommer, Jason.
        Other people's troubles / Jason Sommer.
              p.   cm.—(Phoenix poets)
        ISBN 0–226–76815–5 (alk. paper).—ISBN 0–226–76816–3 (alk. paper)
        I. Title.   II. Series.
        PS3569.0653208   1997   96-48627
        811'.54—dc21   CIP

For Bernardine,
for my parents,
for Matthias, Danielle, and Benjamin

Contents

Acknowledgments

Grateful acknowledgment is made to the editors of the following publications in which these poems, or versions of them, first appeared.

Agni: "The Property of the World"
Alaska Quarterly: "For Whoever Reads My Book in Solitude"
Beloit Poetry Journal: "The Find," "Islanded with Children"
Boulevard: "Last in before Dark"
Delmar: "Lifting the Stone," "Not When You Call Them Do the Pictures Come"
Occident: "Amnesia"
River Styx: "Meyer Tsits and the Children"
Sou'wester: "Aubade"
TriQuarterly: "Adam Naming Himself," "The Wound," "Other People's Troubles," "Mengele Shitting"

I am indebted also to Brenda Walker and Forest Books, Chingford, London, for permission to reprint "Amnesia," "Not When You Call Them Do the Pictures Come," "Meyer Tsits and the Children," "Lifting the Stone," and "Joining the Story," which were collected in *Lifting the Stone,* published in 1991.

The naming of names that follows here can only hint at my gratitude for help received from gifted friends. My deepest thanks to Alan Shapiro for his great generosity; to Jennifer Atkinson, Allison Funk, Jeff Hamilton, Rose Passalacqua, Eric Pankey, Steve Schreiner, Jane O. Wayne, and Jean Wasko for attentive readings, suggestions, and support. Historian David Marwell rendered invaluable assistance. My sincere gratitude goes to Lilly Muller, especially, and to Harry Muller. My wife, Bernardine, provided immeasurable sustenance for these poems and their writer.

OTHER PEOPLE'S TROUBLES

Last in before Dark

Some distance in, a life fills
with people,
despite the early departures—
the childhood friends who must be home
before dark and after a while never
come again,
some of the very old
who were at the gatherings once
or twice, tenderly served and seated
to the side, speaking
their other language sparingly
among themselves—
of those who vanish forever
you may keep a likeness—
but after much coming and going
a life begins to fill,
from the tiny nursery downward—
two figures there, wherever
else they may be,
whose shadows over you
began the night
and day, but now there is
no place for a shadow to fall
that doesn't have shadows
or people in it.

The eave's gutter leads the water away
until the flow is too great
and rises and brims over,
pouring down in front of the windows.
Underneath the rain, the rooms
shelter too many in this, the imagined
occasion, everywhere the constant
and occasional loiter together,
near neighbor and honored guest,
each with something particular to do
with you, an old teacher of yours
who was the first to believe in you,
a woman friend of your wife who exasperates
you in just the way your mother
used to and to whom you are drawn,
your four children with their hundred faces,
an array for each encountered
in every room
under a table, in a closet,
behind the drapes,
taking up spaces, secret or ludicrous,
no one else could.

Inside a great company
and no one expected,
except perhaps the one
whom it seems urgent,
an emergency, to know.
Somehow a space will be made
for such a one,
and all those milling will stand aside
as if into the room a bride comes.
But soon there seems simply no room
for anybody.
The corridors jam with co-workers,
a few college friends, a second wife,
her relatives, the incidental players
from the third city in your life,
a man from whom you get tickets,
a tennis partner.
For months, even years ahead
the boxes in the calendar
contain these known names,

until everyone else must be turned away
no matter who they might be to you,
what promise they hold.
You no longer look—it's impossible,
where could you put them?
And daily you may
brush by people who might stir you,
even meeting a few:
a young man on a train with whom
you really talk about the book
that you are reading.
Where would you put him?
There appeared to be a space
on the second floor
but your dentist is in it,
whom you sometimes see socially,
and where would you put a young man?

Does he have your number?
Do you have his?
Even now there is someone at your door.
How much rarer even than one
whose entry
cannot be denied
like an awaited bride,
more than the sweetness of
the new friend just in before dark,
is the sweetness of you, yourself,
moving through your crowded house
in late afternoon
after rain,
whose life will not fill,
who will answer the door
and make room.

Meyer Tsits and the Children

In the gone world of Roman Vishniac's book
of photographs of Jewish Eastern Europe,
which we sit down to look over,
my father recognizes for certain only
the village idiot of a Munkács neighborhood,
Meyer "Tsits," whom they used to tease:
"Your mother has breasts,"
the children would say as they passed,
and frothing with rage he would give chase
some years before breasts and Meyer were ash.

In the picture, though, Meyer is
contentedly on his way to a meal at the home
of the prosperous burgher who walks beside him
wielding a cane and wearing a *shtreimel*.
(My father thinks the fur hat means it must be *Shabbos*.)
Meyer's benefactor protects the sable tails
from the drizzle with a draped handkerchief
and performing his mitzvah, taking
an unfortunate home to dinner,
he looks more foolish than the fool.

Even in the still one can tell how Meyer moves
on rain-glossed Boco Corsi,
hands tucked into opposite sleeves
making a muff, shuffling the spanceled
steps of a Chinese woman
when Vishniac sights him,
transfers his photographer's gaze down through
the viewfinder of the hidden reflex camera
held at his solar plexus
and out through the lens that peers through
the gap in his overcoat.
In the direction of the background,
straight back until the stacks of firewood,
up stairs behind wrought iron,
through the tiled entry,
rooms burst with Rabinovitz's court
where Hassidim argue passionately
over matters of indifference
to those outside their picture
of the world to come, the Messiah,
and the immortality of the soul.

Out of the book open on a table
in the dining room of this house,
I extend the scale of the photograph
into the world—
and my father's cellar rooms
in 1937 would be somewhere
in the schoolyard of this suburban
New York neighborhood.
But my father would not yet have been there.
Even at the late hour of the photograph,
age fifteen, he welded in Fisher's bike shop
on Kertvarosh, which crosses a few blocks
from where Meyer walks,
and my grandmother Yitta Feiga
still launders clothes in someone's basement.

Vishniac clicks his shutter.
Meyer is caught especially unaware,
after and before—no children near to show him
stripped to his oedipal machinery,
though here in this moment, as in his rage
or his final agony, he was incapable of other modes than candor.

Meyer himself would have survived no selection.
He would have been among the first,
as in 1940 they practiced Holocaust
on his sort just to get the knack.
The picture has been hidden, captured,
liberated, restored while other negatives perished
in the journey from their moments.

My father, who has come through much to get here,
prepares to turn the page.
His own escape and liberation
may not be on his mind now.
There are so many losses and Meyer is little to him,
so few survivals and a picture something but not enough.
The dearest faces to him from then
are faces not in this book,
faces of which there are no extant images
outside of memory.

Meyer Tsits and the children
may not signify to him that before the astounding
cruelties are the ordinary ones,
which have been restored to us at least—
the cruelties of sons and fathers,
cruelties which may be partially redeemed
by forgiveness, and therefore for which
forgiveness is seldom sought,
cruelties not on a street which leads to streets
which lead to the camps
where Meyer still and always in his first
childhood, in his first love and jealousy,
was first for the gas.

I delay with questions the turning of the page.
What does the sign behind them—Mydlow—mean? How old was Meyer?
And it comes to me suddenly that I want
my father to ask forgiveness of Meyer Tsits
for peasant amusements,
for laughing the blank laugh
at those one thinks one never will become,
and that I must ask, too, for having made
some part of his life and death
into coin, capital for speculation.
And to ask forgiveness of Meyer Tsits is to
imagine him restored to faculties
he may never have had,
and to believe for a photographic instant
in the immortality of the soul.

Luck

Since luck came often on her birthday,
at forty-six she was more
prepared than many
when she happened on the store
in the city's renovated market
and in among antiques saw
the tea-server from the set
that Aunt Gerty bought
for her wedding:

the long waist flowed
down with fluting,
the bow-curved handle
like an arm akimbo
tapering to the thinnest join, low
at the side—just the spot
where, knocked from the table
by her running child, its taller partner
for coffee came apart

and, therefore, why it luckily waited
in the shed at first for solder
and now to identify its mate.
Its surfaces danced with lines
in fancies and flourishes almost lost
to the sight in the general shine
but not to the touch. She didn't touch,
just browsed coolly around and left it
for the five minutes it took to find

a phone to call a detective,
to whom the shopkeeper turned in the robber
whom no one would have suspected,
the son of a Doctor
who broke his family's heart
and had the eye of an appraiser
when it came to objets d'art,
household goods and treasures—
who passed up the tumblers that day

of the robbery in favor of several vases,
packing up the older flatware,
the claw-end tongs for sugar
with its four-footed bowl, the tea-server
and more, filling two old suitcases
and making off, finally getting away
with suitcases, crystal, silver,
tongs, bowl, et al. if not
Aunt Gerty's twice-gifted pot.

The Property of the World

The beam that found her, masking her weeping face
suddenly white in the dark room like a searchlight,
should have meant surprise, did surprise
him, the child shuffling from sleep, the fading
bad dream drowned in new alarm at the flash
of the TV on his mother's face—

                         simply
some shot more sky than earth: up through wire
to the watchtowers, the gate's *Arbeit Macht Frei*
arching above in wrought iron, and then
downward the widened light was instead
the limp ivory of limbs, bodies entrenched
and shining out of the ground, a second flare
glimpsed just as he turned.

                              Not yet for him
what will come: a teacher's careful introduction,
the documentary—years ahead—the way
he'll be astonished at this nakedness
which is the property of the world, his eyes
drawn to midpoint, the shock at the undiminished
pubis in the fork of the withered legs.

                              For when
he looked away from her face to see
what she saw, that night it was the shoes,
and only for the moments she allowed
not noticing him there. He saw with her
the shapely heap, the pyramid of shoes
which rose in a mounting absence: antique
high-buttons, work boots, pumps, a small sandal,
all paired invisibly somewhere inside.

Centered in the steady regard of the lens,
the shoes trembled a little. On the abraded
surface of the film, dust leaped back
and forth and a strand of hair appeared, held,
quivering, and whisked away.
                              The light moved most,
though, as the screen changed on her face,
the icy glint of tears gone in shadow,
and in that shadow the deeper shadows passing
were the film's gray blur and blackout turned to shoulders,
backs, heads: a procession of townspeople
to interrupt the dim light of the shoes
in pyramid, of the hair and clothes in bales,
the glitter of granary heaps of eyeglasses,
watches, jewelry. Beneath the cold gaze
of the G.I.s a few of the women in tears, but most
faces of the town composed to show
nothing, as if the blankness were for inscription—
since somewhere it must be written—that those
who need to see these things will not,

and those
who do not need will see them constantly.
Sometimes his mother cried at gatherings
of children: ordinary events at the Jewish school,
the boys and girls in two lines entering
the room, and he would find her weeping eyes—
the child could feel the sympathy that lay
between his mother and some others who
were gone, that stood between his mother
and him, her living child who might have been
among those other children, if everyone
they knew were someone else,
                                    if that could be.
This is his mother's other life and secret,
in which she made a vow, her faithfulness
betrayal to him, as if there were another
child he might have been, a better child
than he has ever been: never sullen,
preferring nothing to a piano lesson,
who wore without demur in summer, long shorts
and knee socks, the sailor coat during winter,
allowed his hair to be cut straight across
his forehead like an English schoolboy's.

Partly on account of that other child
she made her vow about remembering—
and because she wasn't there, but bystanding
here in America in ignorance,
what was it then she had to swear to do
or to forego?—sometimes to put off joy—
to weep without reserve—never to see
without remembering her distant witness
to the story recorded in that shaking light.

She caught sight of him, eager and fearful
at his own looking in, leaped up, hands fluttering:
switching off the set, sweeping her eyes,
taking his hand to lead him back to bed.
Startled at the movement and the sound
the chair made scraping on the floor,

                                    he thought

he heard his father stir in the next room.
His father's sleep is delicate, forbidden
to disturb. He had been somewhere terrible
and narrowly come through, someplace to do
with what was on the films.

                         He might emerge,

disheveled, struggling for focus, looking like anger,
as he once had, naked from the waist,
dark around his genitals like the bodies
in the open graves he nearly was among.
So many dead, how was his father not?
He wondered even as a child,

                           and later,

less than halfway to what he has become,
a man considering memory now, the boy
he was at fifteen could think his father slept
as badly as a Nazi guard should sleep—
and worse—could even say to a friend, that he
had heard of them: men who, as the armies
arrived from east and west, threw away
their uniforms, took on the striped pajamas
of the camps, made Jews of themselves,
stayed in expiation Jews for years,
but could not fully burn away their sins
or what they'd been—which must sometimes have showed.
What could he do, having told a friend
his evil theory? What penance would be sufficient
for such a wrong except to live as a Jew
trying to imagine his father's guiltless life?

From that night he remembers often the shoes
at first, as if the rest were the parts of a dream
forgotten, gradually recovered in
the certainty that there was one night,
no matter if it resembled others, he knows
the one: the light opening and closing on
his mother's face, the people passing, and her
alarm, the screen blackening to a star,
a dot, then nothing, her wiping the stipple of tears
to a glaze high across her cheeks and temples,
giving him the water he asked for, taking
him to his bed, where he heard from their room
the scrape of whispers breaking into voice
and down again to whispers, over and over
before he slept, but nothing of what they said.

Joining the Story

The child's lateness was not yet resistance
to adult demands. He had merely forgotten
time and would be reminded by the hands
of his father who waited, so deep in his own story
of terror and loss that even the angry beating
of his heart was fear. When he saw the boy he joined

the ends of his belt in his hand and rushed to join
his child down the street before resistance
on either part. The child did not see the beating
coming, and if he saw it, he has since forgotten
his father's face then. The setting of his story
was lower: his father's legs, belt, whirling hands

between parked cars, his own warding hands
out of his picture of black curbs, sidewalk-joins,
one glimpse perhaps of a girl in the second story—
people all over the night and no resistance
in the warm air to the sounds of what's been forgotten
long since, some talk, a radio, a quick beating—

minor, and nothing like the beatings
the father got. One of them at the hands
of a young soldier may not be soon forgotten
because he will tell his son, and it will join
those things that are passed on about resistance.
The father struck the soldier in the story.

The man kept spitting in his food. That story
happened in a labor camp, and the beating
was severe, with no chance for more resistance
in a room where they had sticks in their hands,
the first soldier and the others who joined in.
Not killing him, though—perhaps they had not forgotten

some small thing yet, in all they had forgotten.
Later, he'll want the father to recall the story
of his little beating, though how can the son enjoin
him to? He cannot say, On this date my beating
happened—you frightened your son with your hands
and your belt. He knows his father's resistance

to memory. His father has forgotten that beating
when his son, late, took the story from his hands,
joining it after the worst and without resistance.

Lifting the Stone

Not when I call them do the pictures come:
I intend to sleep, and a landscape I never knew
I noted reels by as if seen from a car—
tufted grass backed by a stand of trees,
or a cityscape of gray apartment houses
remembered for no reason that I know of,
not backdrop for events, just incidental
music played between the acts, a scene
to watch as scenes change, till a blurry image
of a wooden shack in New York state somewhere,
equally random-seeming at first, clarifies
as one of the oddly assorted places
my father pointed out for its resemblance
to the hut that he was born in.
                                    I'm nowhere then,
abstracting his story out of its settings,
wanting to think of it as a large stone,
a boulder under which are things I need.
The straw-roofed Czech village, and the camps
with the strung wire through which the dark eyes plead
like droning whole notes on a musical staff,
a diagram of sorrow, are a stone
which I, a Theseus, putting off majority,
can't lift.
            And even imagining I can
takes the forms of my anxious dreaming.
I struggle from room to room in some cold warren

and the class has moved, or Zeyde's deathbed
is in thirty-*four,* a stern attendant says,
as if I should know. So these are the Chinese boxes.
The shrinking gift sequentially deferred,
the expectant rise defeated over and over
by another box. The earth conceals its bulk
until the stone is dug out, hugged up,
and below the stone is another, and under that
again a stone, on down into rooty dirt.
Inside the hole I have not properly pictured
in my mind but which in logic must be there,
I finally come to sword and sandals, but
they are tiny—baby shoes, a toy sword.

Not When You Call Them Do the Pictures Come

In all of his alarm at the late departure
he still had his American thought for the day—
that he might be the only one in Ireland
at that moment who was concerned with time.
He retains the look of what he was doing:
fumbling the keys to the floor, slapping a book
under his arm—considering the lighted radio,
whether it needed extinguishing.
                                        Sometimes he left
it on for hours, a tree falling in the forest
and no one to hear. It might have been playing,
as it often did in his presence, great works
by the masters kept at bay in the background,
spending their largesse almost out of range,
but now it was saying a small country's news.
As he turned away to objects demanding sequence—
the bunched rug in the entry, the door, the lock—

the sounds at the verge of consciousness
became words as the ticking seems in motion toward us
in the dark bedroom, swelling into notice.
Perhaps it was just the syntax leaving till last
that the eight-year-old boy injured in the car
accident on the Naas Road, County Dublin,
in which his father had been killed, the child who was
expected to survive had died that day

which brought it in on him so, in past the simple
machine of his attention. So that he hardly
knew he had heard until he began to cry
for that son, and sat down to be late
for the class he was going to teach, feeling foolish
and yet instructed all over again, by force
as it seems he must be, in what he might have known.

Adam's Call

"Man is the only animal that laughs and weeps: He is . . .
struck with the difference between what things are and what
they ought to be."

—William Hazlitt

Morning it must have been
for the Angel's sword seemed
flame only behind them
turning at the gate.
Also like a blade before them,
the river bending the light
thinly down the ranks of hills
serried each behind the other
cutting then through tawny plains.
On its banks he pauses
to decipher the one feature on the flats,
which at first he thought incised,
creases in the earth:
a dark line splaying into lines
splaying into lines and lines—
scrawled over its own shadow
though, bowed almost to the ground,
wintry even in the heat,
stinted of fruit, of leaf.
It takes him a moment,
which is what it may be to have

a mind for Eden and an eye full of the world,
but then what starts in his belly
shakes his chest,
wind coming from his stretched
mouth, gaped jaws.
Head thrown back he brays
barks crows neighs roars
laughter until tears
channel the dust of his face.
So the animals name him,
and though each now has its own
call, cry, song according to its kind,
one in the hills or circling
unseen in the sun above
gives out with what may be reply.

Adam Naming Himself

Again and again he comes to him—
comes to himself unsummoned

and thinks to himself, I am . . . I will . . .
and it is like the voice

of God in there, the voice in him,
still and strong, not saying

Adam, but I . . . I . . . and not
even really saying,

just there, proposing, considering
out of itself, himself,

over and over without naming,
no stir in surrounding garden.

It is like what the voice of God
will come to later amid

palm trees or brick habitations,
in a desert place or a builded

place, the soundless prompt to become
subject of what ensues,

this, too, given him from the beginning,
that inside him it would be

like what the voice of God descends to,
no one hearing but him.

Amnesia

Wakening late, and light blazed yellow
through curtains and down the pine floorboards
that led from the window to the rush-bottom chair

beside the bed—not a Van Gogh yellow
for I had no Van Gogh anywhere in mind
nor even yellow. The lips formed

by the creases in the sheet were not lips, creases,
or sheet. Each thing surveyed nothing
like anything else, yet everything itself,

exactly, though I had no idea of words.
The stained-glass light blinked several times
blinded by a rising or setting bird

as I can say now but would have been just then
unable to say, calmly unable even
to recover my name or make the room my room

or the body in the bed me, infant, Adam,
clown, anyone who by definition
did not know the use of anything

and might bring sheet to mouth or paw at dust-motes.
As it happened, I only looked, my whole face
feeling as if it were an open eye.

For some minutes, whosoever I was was
breathing in the original light of wakening,
from the belly like a singer: in, quick

as delight, and out—a slow stream that tumbled
from sibilance to something like speech,
and when I knew I had laughed, and thought of it

as the call of a late-dreamer under a sun
high enough to reach over garden trees,
no answer to anything else in creation he'd name,

not the pluck of a nerve, but there in the voice
as a kind of proof that beneath sad facts to come
to say in time was a laugh like a given note

of the earliest music of the animal
who speaks and will remember—I, by then, had
of course already long returned to myself.

Other People's Troubles

The Jewish parable goes
that in the waiting room
where all souls come, they leave
a bundle of their troubles
on hooks. At their return,
emerging from interviews,
they eye the parcels hung
in hundreds on the walls
with care, and take their own.
     *

Trash night, curbside sits
a little sofa meant
for the taking, no one around
even to see our need.
A few speculatable stains,
though in the abstract forest
on its cover, shadows turn out
to be not impeded streetlight
but the body's unguent,
armrests oiled by arms.
We leave the sofa there,
sturdy and recoverable,
life in it yet.
     *

Lilly said that on
the rim of Birkenau,
before the women heard
the name or saw the chimneys'
fires and long shadows
of ash, but after stripping,
herding, shearing, searching,
the unhinged laughter at this,
the only nakedness of its kind
in their lives, a minute
of dribbled shower, the slap
of disinfectant—scalp
crotch and underarms—
the mad clothes thrown at them
without regard for fit,
rag remnants of gowns,
tattered cocktail dresses'
satin, tulle, and crepe
put on—more laughter then:
*Who are these scarecrows who
are us?* But not one of them—
the heavy woman choked
inside the sheath skirt
with the slender girl tenting
in a gown with a train; not
the tall woman bound
in the arms of the short dress,
pulling it down to cover
her thighs, with the small woman
hiking up folds—no one
would trade with anyone.

Mengele Shitting

I

TAKING MY NAME

I walked around New York half-dazed, and what
had happened? Almost nothing, except everything
looked different for the change in a few syllables.

Some hours before, twenty years old, I found out my name
was not my name and wandered, discovering
whatever happens happens in the world

and an altered vision has objects in it:
this octagonal lamppost, that car—
the wrong end of binoculars in their estrangement.

Earlier, the sharp white of a china plate
circumscribing the square of brown honeycake,
laid down by my Aunt Lilly's hand,

which I'd been looking at, seated between my cousins,
when my Uncle Harry—Herschel, Lilly calls him—
started in about my name. I'd breezed in for a meal

from an East Village sublet where I lived on the cheap
with a girl from college, apparently to let
my relatives know just what the thinking was

about the war, who was behind it
and what our demonstrations aimed to do
in addition to airing summer plans to work

driving a cab awhile and go back up to Boston
for some festivals and such. Piqued by something
I said, no doubt, and much about my manner,

my uncle, easy-going usually,
given to after-dinner jokes, laughed suddenly,
tunelessly through thin lips. "Jason Sommer's summer

plans, Jason Sommer, Sommer Sommer," he singsonged.
"You think *that* is your name—*Sommer?*"
"Herschel," Aunt Lilly hissed, as he went on:

"Maybe the man who had it didn't need it
anymore and so your father took it."
"Herschel, *du herst?*" Lilly said.

I wanted to ask him what he meant
but I was used to the etiquette
around survivors. Those who'd been through

the European fire could speak or not,
or any combination of the two. I left—
the evening anyway would not recover

from his tone, which addressed me as American
in a definition other than the one they so desired
for themselves, my uncle and my father,

in Displaced Persons camp, a new definition
Harry learned by living here and having children
for whom he really wanted a softer life than his.

In his voice I was a luxury item no one could afford,
least of all me. He intended this little jolt
I got to be the smallest cost of ignorance

relieved, so much ignorance, so used to it.
But the jolt became a shaking, widening on the subway
home with the hypnotic ticuh-ticuh, ticuh-ticuh

of the train where I remembered a queasy trip
to Canada when at the border I felt my father lie
about his birthplace, his voice odd

as he answered the guard, "Breslau, Germany."
And Harry's melody continued—from every time
I ever heard the faintest hum of what he meant

and what I was now believing, despite my efforts
at reply as I walked under the ordinary signs
enumerating, denominating from walls, store

windows, posts, and poles, seen before and read
on sight, now seen somehow unread.
Harry seemed to say: a person didn't think

and then he did—all I had to do was look around awake,
which is what he learned in hard times even before
the labor camps. As if looking around

had meant anything for Harry when he walked
in front of troops to find landmines and found
no landmines, or when he tried to kill himself

by jumping from a tree and had the branches break
his fall and the fall break his arm, landing
him in dispensary whereby he missed

a fatal deportation. I think that's the story,
which I didn't know then, nor was I so conscious of
how much our own failings trouble us in others,

and especially the young. But he seemed right—
perhaps I hadn't assembled all the evidence
in my possession. I should have known

with what I knew already, or known enough
to ask. Worse still, though, might I have
suspected and pushed away suspicion,

not wanting some ungainly Jewish name,
more easily identifiable even than my face,
ready to say *Jew* before I was ready

to say it? Though I was not in hiding,
or trying for safe haven as far as I am aware,
I also had an alias instead of another name,

more frankly Jewish-sounding,
an alias that properly pronounced
sounds German, is German.

For days after I wasn't who I thought I was
or said I was aloud, at last only curious to know
how many times I would have to see what was familiar

before it became familiar once again,
when I could stop staring at the edges of things
till they shone, outlined in a buzzing light.

Too much trouble to be dizzy with it always,
I might as well have said some peculiarity in the light
of streetlamps, store-front neon, sun or moon

combined with nerves to account for the effect, let light
be light, lamppost, lamppost. It will do if you
can get others to agree that that's the story.

Last year a river flooded through a graveyard.
The bodies, washed away from their stones, recovered
one by one, massed in an unrecoverable

anonymity. The body can shift past its name
or be shifted as mine was. If it happens
it happens to anyone, and I think now I was fortunate

to discover that my name was not mine
as an absolute possession,
to be refreshed in the knowledge

that what has been given me is given
in the grant of other people's survival,
hard won and conferring on them

the power of occasional contempt,
and if the syllables I thought meant me did not,
I can declare them to be me again—as good as any,

mine to make mine for now, can consider
myself sufficiently blessed
that the places of my exile are so close to home.

II

MY FATHER CONCENTRATES ON HIS LUCK

Despite nativity scenes on neighbors' lawns,
it is what we call winter break,
when we are careful and remember,
and I have come home to my parents' house
with my Christian wife and our Jewish children
expecting the usual narrative:
fragments of my father's story
told right to the point of luck.
Ringed by Uzbek soldiers pointing guns,
and they've been shooting people all along,
he's trying to explain without a language
that they understand
that he's no Hungarian, but a Jew.
How do you mime *Jew*
to those with no idea of what a Jew is?
In an old joke the most Asian-looking
would break into Yiddish,
"Jewish? Funny you don't look Jewish,"
but these are only going to shoot until—
as in some old joke
the Red Army Captain—Weinstein—
does save the day in Yiddish,
"*Du bist noch a Yid?*" and in Uzbek,
calling them off, so all that can follow
will follow, eventually even me.

III

SPEAKING OF THE LOST

I cannot look at Lilly as I ask
my father about his younger brother Shmuel,
whom she knew only a little,
the brother also of her husband Harry
sitting on my left. Of these
survivors of slave-labor and war,
her history may be the worst,
and she never speaks of it, not of Auschwitz
or the brothers of her own she lost there,
so it's her eyes I avoid as I break the etiquette
forbidding anyone to ask for speech
when speech is memory and memory is pain.

Alone among them, I try to think of myself
as an adult with a right to speak, a man
who has paid a price and waited long enough,
and I have children of my own, off somewhere
in the house with their mother and my mother,
but I feel like a child demanding a story,
teased with the half-promise of my father's
stories, wanting the one he cannot tell—
the one which has been told to him
by witnesses in that vague way they have
of passing on essentials only, the barest news.

I want whatever else can be recovered
to hold Shmuel at the center of a final scene,
but Harry and my father have begun
now with the boyhood of someone
who is already the hero of a tale—
handsome as he was tall, as strong as he was both,
at home in the forests around Kustanovice,
gifted with understanding the language of animals,
and I continue romance to the end,
imagining him a wild creature,
gnawing his very life away to be free
of the trap, undoing the web of barbed wire
over the window of—not a cattle car,
I knew already—a Karlsruhe freight, one hundred
tons, a number chalked up outside
on the weathered boards, forcing himself
out awkwardly, dropping—how far down?—to the water.

If they suffer memory for me,
maybe I can give them something in return,
the date they need to commemorate
the true anniversary of Shmuel's death
with *yahrzeit* candles—my bookishness of use
to them with S.S. diaries, maps of train routes.
As they grow older, more and more
they want the ritual.
I want the discipline of facts,
about that train to Auschwitz, to anchor Shmuel
in the drift of others' memory where he swims
across an unnamed river to his death
in a flood of gunfire on the farther shore.

I have a plan to follow rivers
if only on the maps, until they intersect
the lines of track, and I will have the place
he died among those crossings.
How many trestle bridges can there be,
crossing as the rivers bend?
I run to get an ordinary atlas,
which shows the possibilities in blue
meandering lines and red lettering:
The Tisza, too soon out of Munkács, or the Latorica,
Laborec, Ondava, Topl'a, Torysa,
as if I could name a river to go back along
against the current of forgetting.
Nervous, I talk and talk, babbling over
the map of Eastern Europe between us on the table:
how, rate by time equaling distance, the date
must lead to the place, but either will give the other,
how at first I thought that it was winter,
filling in with images from movies,
the shot man tumbling down the incline
of the tracks, or rolling into snow.

May Lilly says abruptly *May*
between the twentieth and the twenty-second,
two days, two nights to Auschwitz
from the station at the brickworks.
She was on the transport. She was there.
Nobody looks stunned that she has harbored this
for more than forty years. No voice but mine
determined to recover Shmuel,
to rescue the hero from her silence.
How could she have kept it all these years?
Lilly, there was shooting. The train was halted
on a trestle bridge—think, the twentieth,
the twenty-first, day or night?—
Brakes shrieking. *Polizei* shouting in German.
The splashing below in the water.
Surely she would recall which day that was?
No, says Lilly mildly, *there was shooting*
many times, many times the train would stop
without a reason. In our car, everyone,
old people and children, pressed together.
The women held rags out of the window to catch
rainwater we could drink. The train had many cars.
No one thing happened I could tell from where I was.

IV

Aunt Lilly, Lilly, *Liteshu*
your sisters called you sometimes

in those heavy accents.
Like all of those connected

to my father, you had several names
in the several languages

of the old region, most had
American names, too.

No one had more names than my father
since he had been on the run.

Lilly, I wanted to give you something
for my bad thoughts as a child,

my conjuring with your name
when I tried to give a name

to fear—precocious research
in Ginzberg's *Legends of the Jews*

and I had you in with Lilith,
Jewish bogey woman

from Babylonian originals
Lilit, Lilu.

She was Adam's
before the mother

of us all. Just as my father's brother,
mild Herschel, Uncle Harry,

was no match for you,
Lilith was stronger than Adam,

first wife, fierce and sexy,
who left him flat in an argument

over who got the top in copulation,
flying off to breed demons

from nocturnal emissions, screeching
in the *Lilah,* semitic night,

against whom grandmothers incanted
and posted protective charms

to save the infants
over whom she had power.

*   *   *   *   *

I thought you might kill children,
you had such anger. *Shmutz! Shmutz!*
you screamed down the street
at your son Steven
who would pick up junk
from the gutter or
the garbage cans—

an oily piece of a sparkplug,
smacked from his hand—
Dirt! Dirt!—
the guts of a music box,
the head of a doll,
lead weights inside to tip the eyes
open and shut.

I took things from him,
anyone could.
He was available to force,
one of those people who limply
allowed so much
it was a challenge
not to bully him.

He was a version
of what I would understand
a Jew to be.
His may have been the first
life in which I was a bystander.
The two of us, small boys,
the women chattering away

around us on the sidewalk
of St. John's Place in Brooklyn.
You took him between parked cars—
the matter-of-fact, casual
power of it!—
down with his pants,
you tickled his penis and he peed.

*   *   *   *   *

Something was owed you for what
had been taken, and what had been taken?

Your mother and father, four brothers,
grandparents, uncles, aunts, cousins,

most of the family and every thing,
any love that might be unafraid,

the momentum of the everyday,
sleeping along too deeply even to dream

catastrophe. What was owed
in compensation, then?

Whatever could be restored.
Your sisters. Whatever came after

that would compensate. A husband
from a fiancé who survived,

children to be named for the dead. Who owed it?
God, the Germans, the children themselves.

Was it paid? Herschel returned,
the Germans gave some money,

children were given, and given
the names of the dead. No.

*   *   *   *   *

I, too, have something insufficient to give,
a complicated gift likely to give offense,
or perhaps no gift at all
since I hope you'll never see these words.
Your pardon, Lilly, anyway
for bringing these things up again,
also for retelling
what you know better than anyone,
out here where others listen,
as if it were something of my own.

But what I have for you
that you will not have heard,
even if you kept up with news
disinterred about the camps,
a dark gleam of shards
embedded in the midden of the rest,
concerns the later life
of the murderous Doctor Mengele
who selected you for life
on the ramp at Auschwitz-Birkenau

within several moments
of sending to the gas
your parents and small brother.
I have the story from a dear man,
the most reliable of witnesses,
who has held Mengele's bones
in his own hands—
the bastard *is* dead, Lilly,
the best evidence indicates.
The bastard. The monster.

*   *   *   *   *

There may be hints that God exists in some diminished form, humorous.

At the railhead Lilly saw him first, the binary motion of the stick,
among the stumbling shoals *raus*ed from the boxcars,
doling general death and fishing for his special interests—
twins, any anomaly: the hunchback father and clubfooted son—
unrhythmic metronome sending people to the left or right
onto different lines—death,   life,   death,   death, death death,   death—
or with a jerk of the thumb, a flick of the finger in white kid gloves,
arms in a half embrace of himself, left arm across his waist propping
the right, which moved only from the wrist as he parted the living stream,
fingertip flick of the finger, jerk of the thumb, or conducting with that baton,
humming opera, *tall* Lilly thought and *handsome,* in his monocle
    and gloves—
not merely handsome, courtly in the way my aunt described him.

Because survivors say some of the worst of the dailiness
the S.S. enforced involved the bowels,
because in terror of the latrines at night or too weak or diarrheal anyway,
people relieved themselves in the precious containers they used for soup,
or, kept at attention for hours at roll call, soiled themselves where
    they stood—
or at the work details, no break provided, and begging requests refused—

bear with me, Lilly, there is a reason for the coprology, and this is it:
Years later after his brief internment, every day a new name when
    the Americans
called the roll, after his release undetected and all the years of names,
Ullman, Holman, Gregor, Gregori, Hochbicler, Gerhard, Alvez, and the rest,
he acquired the habit, a kind of grooming out of fear, of biting on his
    moustache-ends,
severing bits of hair and swallowing, but since he was not animal enough
    to cough it up,
the hair lodged in his lower bowel and grew and grew as he kept chewing
until it valved the passage closed with a hairball, *tricho-bezoar,*
an asylum condition usually of the stomach—but in this case happily
    otherwise.
So Mengele shitting would have to lean forward with his precise fingers
    in his rectum
to guide stools past, sometimes, of course, not stools but a pouring
    over his hands,
hot as his own insides, bathing him as he should be bathed.

Lilly, rejoice in what he felt arriving at the dispensary in Jundiai, Brazil,
the filth of the surroundings bad enough (the town itself, the outer office)—
a surgeon, too, to shudder at, small-town absurd in cowboy boots,
but worst of all when he reached the sanctum of the operating room,
    around the walls
he saw disposable rubber gloves adhering to tiles, drying for re-use. But
    he had little choice.
Here he would be cut open to get at what he thought was cancer.

So, Lilly, a kind of symmetry that will pass for justice in its absence,
irony's schadenfreude, ours by interpretation of what occurs,
as good as construing Providence out of the luck of chance survival—
yours, say, Harry's, or my father's—or constructing a God
who happens to care for some and takes care of others with a little quittance.
In Dante effluvia doesn't seem that much, serious enough for the *Inferno*—
Canto 18, Ring 8, Trench 2—frauds swim it.
Who would wish for hell just to have Mengele in it?
What Mengele did was not done to him, nothing was done to him by anyone,
but he was unhappy, abandoned, fearful, startled at the least sound:
a car backfiring, being addressed by someone unexpectedly—
a small hell in the body, such as the innocent also experience,
and that hand, which motioned thousands toward death,
those fingers reaching up his ass for years,
this thing I tell you that few people know.

Islanded with Children

I dreamt a palimpsest of beach
written on and waved clear,
a place I stand and teach
from memory a Hebrew prayer.

Islanded, with sons and daughter,
we are escaped alone
sole remnant of a slaughter
till other children come

from islands of their own,
left out of Creation
only in a late account,
across the fringe of tide,

two by two at first,
but numbers do not mount:
some leave as more arrive.
The children chorus like the surf,

song raggedly begun
ends in a partial unison
and starts again. My daughter rocks,
repeating the notes I substituted,

the words I used instead
of those that I forgot,
to others who teach others
to their left the chanted song

in which I just discern my errors
before the singing changes further,
my own part almost gone,
the children almost strangers

until the first one comes
who is, who only knows the sounds
he hears are sounds of prayer, or were.

The Find

for my son, Matthias

For days, all day the sounds we could not place—
above us sometimes, sometimes underground,
the smallest fragments of a newborn wail.
No human baby nearby, a kitten somewhere,
lodged in the house's body, we settled on—
and searched, straining at first to hear the cries
but then, now that we had the tune, we heard
its faintest whispers. Even when we didn't
we felt that soon we would, and so we did:
the first day and the second. The third day
was mostly interval, and we reprised
the rounds of everywhere we'd thought to look,
no one more intent than you at going
anywhere the sound appeared to lead.
That summer you'd begun to muster cool
against intrusion, holding yourself apart
from all of us, building over what
you were, that sweetest, most forthcoming child,
in long muscle and silence. Offended when
I kept you from the sloping wooden ladder
to the roof, you brought a flashlight to the basement,
stamping downstairs. You let your interest
resume its technical expression: pleased

at the sub- and superstructure of the house,
basement and attic, places of pipes and struts
and wires, finding what offers and disguises
access: hatches, grills, and gratings; inspecting
vents and ducts.
                  When night came no one had heard
the animal for hours, and I prepared
us for defeat, wanting to hide this one
mortality at least. I said what we thought
weak cries within were stronger, but from outside
and at a distance, that it had been rescued
by its mother. Nobody was convinced.
And then the slimmest filaments of call
did lead outside, behind the house, under
the long porch, which I probed with light.
You took the flashlight and crawled in. We waited,
our shins brushed occasionally by the beams,
listening to the fricatives of crawl—
the scrape and sweep, sent into flurries
by more new pulses of beacon mewing—
followed by another sound, the purest
vocative, halfway between an Oh
and Ah, high-pitched, descending, all trail
and aftersound, wind-down and exhalation,
stretching the time it took to say itself,
to say you, since it was yours, was you,
and is—you constant, Ah covert you,
you heart's cry in answer, you for whom
I didn't know I waited—go in and I
will wait for you again always now,
you emerging suddenly, steadily,
with the bundled life riding on your palm,
already something muted in your pride.

In the Rush Hour

Space opens in the traffic, one car coming only
and at sufficient distance—
although he seems to speed to close the gap, we go—
the car beside and I.

A block ahead the light dams back two lines, nowhere
to go but to their end.
The driver behind me, though, leans on the horn and holds
the blare right to my bumper.

Carefully I lean forward to mouth into the mirror,
but stop at what I see.
Behind, already raging, chopping toward the glass
rhythmic with obscenities,

hissing and striking the words, the thin face so distorted
I hardly recognize
a woman whom I know: a friend of my wife's and mine,
someone for whom I'd written

a letter of recommendation. That we had "broken bread
together" in just those words
recurred to me absurdly. I began to laugh,
and tried to project my laughter

back to her through the mirror. I pointed at myself,
waved, gestured the ways
I thought distinct from anger, all the time speaking to her
saying who I was.

But the furious words went on, and she would not meet my eyes.
I felt some kind of chill
and wrote her name in pencil on a yellow legal pad,
big block letters scored

as black as I could make them and turned them toward her.
Her car still rocked with fury.
As we crept closer to the light, she'd leave a moment's gap
then drive straight at my back,

to stop short over and over. Once through the intersection,
tailgating dangerously,
she followed until she had to turn away, a quick veer
onto another road.

I feel I have to tell her about the way I saw her,
what she was, or could be—
I know that when I do, it will be jocular,
teasing just a little,

so I can tell her without also saying how afraid
I was that she *did* know me,
that for reasons of my own I am ready to believe
in rage that can make strangers

out of anyone, that even those who might know
each other uncontorted
will fail to find resemblance to the familiar face
along a road somewhere,

that however this becomes an anecdote out of the city,
beneath our smiling then,
my laughter, her taking all of it in good part,
will lie the other face.

Aubade

As I came from the lot
of the only open store
at this lightly trafficked hour
to wait at the light,
pulling in behind

him, first I thought
he was trying out a pick-up line,
the young man in the red car
leaning toward
the woman in the white.

He fairly poured
his words at her, and then
I saw the glass between them.
The windows up,
how could he hope

that she would understand him?
And yet she did: *beautiful*
the word
even in profile
I could see he said.

She smiled
and made her brief reply,
a little shy of rhapsody.
We drove away in tandem.
They met at every light and sign

for several miles,
stopping side by side.
They laughed and shook
their heads in wonder
at themselves or simply looked,

one turning then the other.
Once they turned together
like someone in a mirror.
Closed windows made a kind of sense
of the dumbshow extravagance.

Just as actors, masked,
must amplify
gesture and speech,
lovers magnify
ways they must memorably

be seen to feel, to reach
each other past
the separations:
space, glassy silence,
the difference

in their destinations.
Last stop before the highway,
before she had to turn away,
she quickly mimed a telephone.
He pressed

his fingers to his lips
and to the glass,
she arced a kiss
to him along the airwaves,
and each of us went on alone.

The Wound

1.

Not dressing it, but dressed
for it, bright colors to distract
those few who might suspect
the thing that she possessed.

Beneath her clothes, of course,
it lay, invisible
in spite of what she thought,
no telling bruise to heal,

and always keeping silent—
her talk became a sort
of music of concealment.

2.

As in an accident,

no father fierce to others
no mother tender to her
could ever have prevented
what memory would harbor.

3.

When most invisible
she felt it start to swell
out through the mediums
between herself and others,

as if it were a sound
ringing through air and water,
and soon the swelling was
that nearly everyone

became in part the one
who'd given her the wound.

4.

Think of the emptiness
where only light will carry,

of her as planetary—
as perigee, apogee
her approach and withdrawal,
and that tremble besides

at that same certain distance
that made you theorize
about some unseen presence
exerting gravity.

Despite—because of—all,
moved by her, you conclude
this much concerning what
she would revolve around.

Not you. But not the wound.

For Whoever Reads My Book in Solitude

After the week, after some music, the news,
this night my reader ends the day with me.
The voice is not aloud and neither self
nor other fully, speaking for an hour only
the better part of what I did intend,
along with what I half remember dreaming,
and other things—some of which may concern
these eyes that move across the same place twice,
the face frowning, but now with half a nod
the page turns.
                    "One sun in one thousand windows"
are the words, and for her perhaps a harborside:
a path of light leads down to the sun sinking
in a bay, one sun in a thousand waves,
and when she turns—the surfaces of windows,
ruddy until the lights come on inside.

My reader pauses, looks up at the lamp,
and over toward the window of which the dark
has made a mirror giving back an arm
of the armchair, her shoulder, the lamp.
She settles in again, lips almost moving
from time to time. The pages turn and the head

slightly, eyes searching for the start
of what comes next. Brows arched, one page she reads
over and over, then goes on, unfurrowing,
to where, suddenly grown still, the stillest
yet, so that nothing moves, only the iamb
of pulse at her temple, tapping also
in her crossed-over leg, trembling the book.
After a little while my reader rises.
Putting the book down, she drifts slowly out,
returns and shuts the light, picks up the book
and takes it with her down the corridor.

Horizon with Sun

It must be warm there
on the horizon,
so much closer to the sun
setting or rising,

a promise of convergence where,
due west or east,
the conjoined margins
of the road

can be envisioned
like rails to meet
at that point in the illusion
in which infinite distances

become enclosed.
Despite the semblances
of sunset or sunrise
what could it be but noon,

if we did arrive,
surmounting the curve
of all appearances?
We, by whom

I mean lovers in their pairs,
also each of us alone,
any whose differences diverge
in views of where

horizon appears to border
air and earth or water
and what horizon signifies
by reaching the limit

of what can be perceived or known,
still harboring events
just on or over it
thereby considered imminent.

So of the figures shown
to rest on the continuum
of longing might one
represent the will,

divided into both
expectancy itself
and equally the opposite?
Emblems aside,

in the occurrence
we do relinquish forms of hope
to flicker for an instant
satisfied

before we understand
what we allowed ourselves to think—.
that anything could happen
when nothing has,

that where we were was
somewhere else,
while elsewhere again:
a thin sun

moves upon the brink
of fall or rise
and we feel the familiar chill,
measured in blue distance

from the place we stand
to the horizon.